W9-CPN-559

WITHDRAWN

No longer the property of the
Boston Public Library.
Sale of this material benefits the Library.

THE GOOD LIFE
ACCORDING TO
HEMINGWAY

ALSO BY A. E. HOTCHNER

Fiction

Louisiana Purchase
The Man Who Lived at the Ritz
Treasure
The Dangerous American

Nonfiction

The Boyhood Memoirs of A. E. Hotchner
Dear Papa, Dear Hotch
Everyone Comes to Elaine's
Shameless Exploitation in Pursuit of the Common Good
   (with Paul Newman)
The Day I Fired Alan Ladd
Choice People
Hemingway and His World
Doris Day
King of the Hill
Looking for Miracles
Sophia, Living and Loving
After the Storm
Blown Away
Papa Hemingway

THE GOOD LIFE

ACCORDING TO

HEMINGWAY

EDITED BY

A. E. HOTCHNER

ecco

An Imprint of HarperCollinsPublishers

THE GOOD LIFE ACCORDING TO HEMINGWAY. Copyright © 2008 by A. E. Hotchner. All rights reserved. Printed in the United States of America. No part of this book may be used or reproduced in any manner whatsoever without written permission except in the case of brief quotations embodied in critical articles and reviews. For information, address HarperCollins Publishers, 10 East 53rd Street, New York, NY 10022.

HarperCollins books may be purchased for educational, business, or sales promotional use. For information, please write: Special Markets Department, HarperCollins Publishers, 10 East 53rd Street, New York, NY 10022.

An extension of this copyright page appears on page 125.

FIRST EDITION

Designed by Ralph Fowler / rlf design

Library of Congress Cataloging-in-Publication Data is available upon request.

ISBN: 978-0-06-144489-0

08   09   10   11   12   ID/RRD   10   9   8   7   6   5   4   3   2   1

Previous page: At Finca Vigía. Opposite: On safari with white hunters, Philip Perceval (at left), and his son, Richard.

To the memory of my good friend

Jack Hemingway

CONTENTS

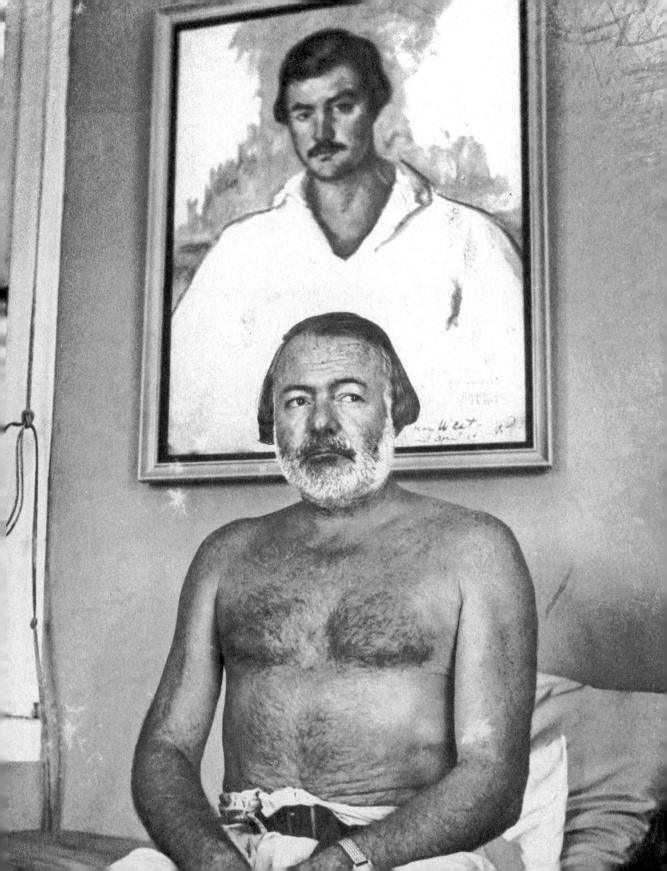

FOREWORD

I first met Ernest Hemingway in the winter of 1948, when, as a literary bounty hunter, I was sent by a magazine to Havana to ask him to write an asinine essay. I had become a bounty hunter because, at the conclusion of my four-year service in the Air Force, bloated with severance pay, I had elected to be discharged in Paris, where the dollar ruled supreme and where I was enjoying a romantic relationship with a young lyric soprano of the Paris Opera who had proposed cohabitation at her place in Neuilly.

The only problem with this nirvana was that while I was reveling in my Paris excesses, the editorial jobs that possibly could have been mine were quickly being filled by diligent military personnel who had been promptly discharged in the States. My friend Arthur Gordon, who had been in the Air Force with me, had become editor of *Cosmopolitan*, then a reputable literary magazine, before its corruption by Helen Gurley Brown, during my two years of Parisian frolic had several times offered me an editorial position, but when I finally did return to the States, my finances having dwindled to the price of a cabin-class ticket on the *Ile de France*, neither Arthur nor any other editor had an opening for ex–Major Hotchner, lately a bon vivant of avenue Neuilly.

Faced with the alarming prospect of having to return to the St. Louis law firm from which my draft board had extricated me, Arthur, a very compassionate man, out of pity invented a job for me: he gave me a list of

Opposite: Hunting with Hotchner, Ketchum, Idaho, 1956.

writers who had written for *Cosmo* during its long, illustrious past, with the understanding that I would seek them out and attempt to induce them again to contribute to the magazine. The list was intimidating: Dorothy Parker, Sinclair Lewis, John Steinbeck, Edna Ferber, James Thurber, Pearl Buck, Fannie Hurst, Ernest Hemingway, John O'Hara, William Faulkner, Robert Benchley—a roll call of the most important writers of their time. My remuneration would be expenses plus a $300 bonus for every writer I bagged. It wasn't much, but it was either skimp along on that, or slink back to St. Louis and that affiliation I had grandly renounced (after less than two years of practice) with the firm of Taylor, Mayer, Shifrin and Willer.

At first it was daunting to contact the prestigious names on my bounty list and convince them to write something for old times' sake, but to my surprise, I found that writers of their stature were almost never invited to write for specific publications; rather, they sent their compositions to their agents or directly to their publishers. Famous though they were, some of those on my list were flattered by the attention, and as a result I did have some success. Dorothy Parker, sadly in need of income, not only wrote a short story about a deadly game of charades, but remained a good friend until her death many years later. Edna Ferber had been "frozen" (her word) since the atrocities in Germany, but she too broke the ice and wrote a story; like Dorothy, she continued to stay in touch with me for years afterward. In fact, a few months after our initial meeting at her apartment in the Sherry-Netherland in New York City, she invited me to a memorable dinner she hosted, which was attended by George Kaufman, Moss Hart, Alexander Woollcott, Kitty Carlisle, Groucho Marx, Mary Astor, Helen Hayes, and Robert Benchley. Of those on my bounty list, only John O'Hara and William Faulkner dismissed me abruptly.

The one name on the list I did not attempt to contact was Hemingway. For me, he was more formidable than the others, not only as a writer but also as a prestigious member of the celebrity echelon of that time. His exploits—shooting wild beasts on safari, fishing the high seas, involving himself in the world of bullfighting—were widely covered in the media, often with considerable exaggeration. (As I write this, I am reminded of an incident that occurred years later when we were having a drink at the bar of the Stork Club, prior to being seated in the exclusive Cub Room by the proprietor, Sherman Billingsley. An inebriated gentleman detached himself from his group at the end of the bar and swayed over to Hemingway, his drink hoisted in toast position. "You know who the three most important people in America are?" he asked slurringly. "General Eisenhower, Ernest Hemingway, and Tom Collins!")

I had been in awe of Hemingway ever since Hilda Levy, my high school English teacher, introduced me to Hemingway's autobiographical Nick Adams stories. My favorite was a story called "The Battler," which, as it turned out, I was destined to dramatize twenty years later for NBC's *Playwrights '56*, which initiated me as a playwright, as well as the young actor Paul Newman, who played the lead. I had read all of Hemingway's books and seen the movies allegedly based on them. In fact, during the war, I had seen *For Whom the Bell Tolls*, starring Gary Cooper and Ingrid Bergman, in a hangar in Tripoli where my outfit, the 13th Wing of the Air Force Anti-Submarine Command, was stationed.

"Why haven't you contacted Ernest Hemingway?" Arthur wanted to know. "*Cosmo* ran a section of *To Have and Have Not* in advance of its publication, so we're on friendly grounds."

"But, Arthur, you want me to ask him to write an article on the future of literature—I can't ask the great Hemingway to write something as dumb as that. He'll level me."

"It's part of a series—Frank Lloyd Wright on the future of architecture, Eugene O'Neill on drama, Henry Ford II on automobiles, Balanchine on ballet, and so forth. Distinguished company. Don't be a coward. Get your freckled ass down to Cuba or you'll be back in St. Louis with your nose buried in a *Corpus Juris Secundum*."

When I arrived in Havana in 1948, I took the coward's way out and wrote a note to Hemingway, telling him that I was there on an embarrassing assignment, to request that he write an article on the future of literature. Would he please send me a turndown so I could keep my miserable job at *Cosmopolitan*? I arranged for a messenger from the Nacional Hotel, where I was staying, to deliver my note to Hemingway's place in San Francisco de Paula, a little village on the outskirts of Havana.

That afternoon, the phone in my room rang and a hearty voice said, "This Hotchner? Dr. Hemingway here. Got your note. Can't let you abort your mission, or you'll lose face with the Hearst organization, which is about like getting bounced from a leper colony. You want to have a drink around five? There's a bar called La Florida. Just tell the taxi."

Thus began what became an adventurous friendship that endured until his death, fourteen years later, a friendship I chronicled in my memoir, *Papa Hemingway*. A collection of all of our letters, *Dear Papa, Dear Hotch*, recently published, contains the early letters we exchanged after that initial trip. Ernest did indeed write something for *Cosmo*, not the article on literature's future but a work of fiction that began as a short story and morphed into a novel, *Across the River and into the Trees*. By then Arthur had created a spot for me on the magazine's staff and I accompanied Ernest to Paris and Venice to fact-check certain passages in the manuscript.

When Arthur was fired, however, and replaced by Herbert Mayes, a repulsive, egomaniacal, tasteless man who was editor of *Good Housekeeping*, I quickly left the magazine and entered the precarious ranks of the freelancers, never again to be respectably employed. Precarious existence though it was, freelancing enabled me to do whatever I wanted to do, and go wherever I wanted to go, often on adventures with Ernest. In Paris, attending the fall meet of the Auteuil steeplechase, which culminated in a great windfall that stoked an opulent Christmas; in Cuba, fishing for marlin in the waters beyond the Morro Castle; in Spain, running with the bulls in Pamplona and following the mano-a-mano rivalry between Ordóñez and Dominguín; in Ketchum, hunting pheasants and mallards; in New York, attending the fights and the World Series at Yankee Stadium. Many of our meetings, like the week we spent at his house in Key West, related to my dramatizations of his novels and short stories.

Everywhere we went, Ernest's conversations with me and with his friends and strangers along the way, his observations about himself, about the behavior of others, including animals, fish, and birds, about the world around him, were so remarkable I felt compelled to jot them down, often on myriad pieces of paper—hotel stationery, paper napkins, menus, notepads, the back of laundry lists. Ernest was a vibrant conversationalist, funny, wise, argumentative and fiercely opinionated, an extraordinary raconteur with acute recall of people and events from his earliest boyhood on.

I included some of his observations and ruminations—wise, funny, bitchy, cruel, philosophical, sad, revelatory—in *Papa Hemingway*, but when I excised more than one hundred pages from the first draft of the manuscript, many of those quotations did not appear in the published edition. Now I have included his wit and wisdom from both the published version and the cut pages in this collection, along with the accumulation of those scraps of paper that I had stored in a bottom drawer of my desk.

Many of the quotes in this book emanated from Ernest's conversations with people we met up with during our travels: Gary Cooper in Ketchum; Robert Graves in Churriana, Spain; Lauren Bacall in Málaga; Charles Scribner Sr. in New York; Charles Ritz in Paris; Adriana Ivancich, the young Italian aristocrat, in Venice; Marlene Dietrich in New York; Ingrid Bergman in Milan; Cipriani in Harry's Bar, Venice; Gigi Viertel in Paris and Venice; Bill and Annie Davis traveling throughout Spain; Toots Shor in New York; General Buck Lanham and the Maharajah of Cooch Behar in Churriana; high school students in Hailey, Idaho; George Plimpton in Madrid; Slim Hayward (Lady Keith) in Pamplona; the renowned artist Waldo Peirce in Nevada; Ava Gardner in the Escorial; Count Federico Kechler in Venice.

To my knowledge, none of these entries has appeared in any of Ernest's published works, but he often repeated himself, especially in his later years, so it is entirely possible that in his conversation he expressed thoughts similar to those he had previously written about in his books.

The sum total of these diverse quotations is a virtual portrait of Ernest that has eluded the numerous biographies that have been published since his death. None has really captured the mercurial, profound, contradictory, passionate, disparaging, effusive personality as revealed in his own observations about the joys, the sorrows, the injustices, the glory of the world in which he lived.

—A. E. Hotchner

WRITING

When a man has the ability

to write and the desire to write,

no critic can damage his work if

it is good, or save it if it is bad.

In the beginning I was not making any money at it, and I just wrote as well as I could—the editors didn't like it, but someday they would. I really didn't care about criticism. The best thing about your early days is that you are not noticed. You don't have to deal with criticism, and you really enjoy your workdays. You think it's easy to write and you feel wonderful, but you're not thinking about the reader, who is not having much enjoyment. But when you start to mature and begin to write for the reader, writing becomes more difficult. In fact, when you look back on anything you've written, what you recall is what a tough go it was. Every day the rejected manuscripts would come back through the slot in the door of that bare room where I lived over the Montmartre sawmill. They'd fall through the slot onto the wood floor, and clipped to them was that most savage of all reprimands—the printed rejection slip. The rejection slip is very hard to take on an empty stomach, and there were times when I'd sit at that old wooden table and read one of those cold slips that had been attached to a story I had loved and worked on very hard and believed in, and I couldn't help crying. When the hurt is bad enough, I cry.

When a writer first starts out, he gets a big kick from the stuff he does, and the reader doesn't get any; then, after a while, the writer gets a little kick and the reader gets a little kick; and, finally, if the writer's any good, he doesn't get any kick at all and the reader gets everything.

There are only two absolutes I know about writing: one is that if you make love while you are jamming on a novel, you are in danger of leaving the best parts of it in the bed; the other is that integrity in a writer is like virginity in a woman—once lost, it is never recovered.

Previous page: At his home, San Francisco de Paula, Cuba. Opposite: City room at the Kansas City Star.

Fiction is inventing out of what knowledge you have. If you invent successfully it is more true than if you try to remember it.

Contrary to the professors' published reports, my first job on the *Kansas City Star* was to find the labor reporter in one of several drinking haunts, get him sobered in a Turkish bath, and get him to a typewriter. So if the professors really want to know what I learned on the *Star*, that's what I learned. How to sober up rummies.

This is where I wrote *The Snows of Kilimanjaro*, upstairs here [Key West], and that's as good as I've any right to be. Pauline and I had just come back from Africa, and when we hit New York, the newsboys asked me what my next project was, and I said to work hard and earn enough money to get back to Africa. It ran in the papers that way and a woman who read it got in touch with me and asked me to have a drink with her. Very classy society woman, extremely wealthy, damn attractive. We had good martini conversation and she said if I wanted to return to Africa so badly, why put it off just for money when she would be very happy to go with me and my wife and foot the bill. I liked her very much and appreciated the offer but refused it. By the time we got down here to Key West, I had given a lot of thought to her and the offer and how it might be if I accepted an offer like that. What it might do to a character like me whose failings I know and have taken many soundings on. Never wrote so directly about myself as in that story. The man is dying, and I got that pretty good, complete with handles, because I had been breathed upon by the Grim Reaper more than once and could write about that from the inside out.

In my opinion, the Hemingway influence on writing is only a certain clarification of the language which is now in the public domain.

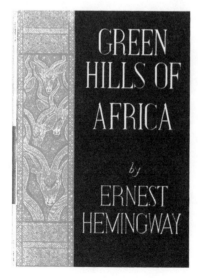

I learned how to make a landscape from Mr. Paul Cézanne by viewing his paintings at the Luxembourg Museum a thousand times on an empty gut, and I am pretty sure that if Mr. Paul was around, he would like the way I write them and be happy that I learned it from him.

Opposite: Original book covers (left to right), Scribner's, 1935; Scribner's, 1940. Above: The house and pool, Key West, Florida, 1955.

Never yet sold a share of stock I bought, never had to. I can ride out any depression as long as they put me in a chair and give me a pencil and paper.

A book you talk about is a book you don't write.

A big lie is more plausible than truth. People who write fiction, if they had not taken it up, might have become very successful liars. As they get further and further away from a war they have taken part in, all men have a tendency to make it more as they wish it had been rather than how it really was.

After you finish a book, you're dead. But no one knows you're dead. All they see is the irresponsibility that comes in after the terrible responsibility of writing.

The test of a book is how much good stuff you can throw away.

When I'm working on a book I try to write every day except Sunday. I don't work on Sunday. It's very bad luck to work on a Sunday. Sometimes I do, but it's bad luck just the same.

A serious writer is not to be confused with a solemn writer. A serious writer may be a hawk or a buzzard or even a popinjay, but a solemn writer is always a bloody owl.

I like to write standing up to reduce the old belly and because you have more vitality on your feet. Who ever went ten rounds sitting on his ass? I write description in longhand because that's hardest for me and you're closer to the paper when you work by hand, but I use the typewriter for dialogue because people speak like a typewriter works.

Opposite: On safari, 1953. Left: Original book covers (left to right), Scribner's, 1937; Scribner's, 1926. Following page: At his work desk, Cuba, with his favorite cat, Crazy Christian.

It's all so beautiful in this misty light. Mr. Degas could have painted it and gotten the light so that it would be truer on his canvas than what we now see. That is what the artist must do. On canvas or on printed page, he must capture the thing so truly that its magnification will endure. That is the difference between journalism and literature. There is very little literature. Much less than we think.

I have always made things stick that I wanted to stick. I've never kept notes or a journal. I just push the recall button and there it is. If it isn't there, it wasn't worth keeping.

Previous page: At his work desk, Cuba, with his favorite cat, Crazy Christian. Below: With a wounded owl, Ketchum, Idaho.

The country that a novelist writes about is the country he knows, and the country that he knows is in his heart.

I'm the kind of writer who can discard a sheet of manuscript paper without crumpling it up into a ball.

Back in the days when American billboard advertising was in flower, there were two slogans that I always rated above all others: the old Cremo Cigar ad that proclaimed, "Spit Is a Horrid Word—but Worse on the End of Your Cigar," and "Drink Schlitz in Brown Bottles and Avoid That Skunk Taste." You don't get creative writing like that anymore.

I like to start early, before I can be distracted by people and events, and I start by rereading and editing everything I have written to the point I left off. That way I go through a book I'm writing several hundred times. Then I go right on, no pissing around, crumpling up paper, pacing, because I always stop at a point where I know precisely what's going to happen next. So I don't have to crank up every day. Most writers slough off the toughest but most important part of their trade—editing their stuff, honing it and honing it until it gets an edge like the bullfighter's *estoque*, the killing sword. One time my son Patrick brought me a story and asked me to edit it for him. I went over it carefully and changed one word. "But, Papa," Mousy said, "you've only changed one word." I said, "If it's the right word, that's a lot."

There are no contemporary themes. The themes have always been love, lack of it, death and its occasional temporary avoidance which we describe as life, the immortality or lack of immortality of the soul, money, honor and politics.

There is no friend as loyal as a book.

Above: With son Patrick. Opposite: Ernest liked to write standing up in his bedroom.

I logged a lot of reading time on the S.S. *Africa* and reread *Huckleberry Fin*, which I have always touted as the best American book ever written and which I still think is. But I had not read it for a long time, and this time reading it, there were at least forty paragraphs I wished I could fix. And a lot of the wonderful stuff you remember, you discover you put there yourself.

I had a lot of requests to write fight stories, but I have always tried to write only one story on anything if I got what I was after the first time, because there was a hell of a lot I wanted to write about and I knew even then that the clock runs faster than the pen.

In order to write about life, first you must live it!

I have never learned anything from the critics. In this book [*Across the River and into the Trees*] I moved into calculus, having started with straight math, then moved to geometry, then algebra. The next time out it will be trigonometry. If they don't understand that, to hell with them.

I hate plays. Did you ever listen to the dialogue of a play with your eyes shut?

You invent a novel from what you know, from all the things you've ever learned— and then you write it down, as if you're telling the story to yourself or to your kids.

Many people regard writing as an easy way to become rich and famous. All you need is a perfect ear, absolute pitch, the devotion to your work that a priest of God has for his, the guts of a burglar, no conscience except to writing, and you're in. It's easy. Never give it a thought. Many people have a compulsion to write. There is no law against it, and doing it makes them happy while they do it and presumably relieves them. But the compulsory writer should be advised not to. Should he make the attempt, he might well suffer the fate of the compulsive architect, which is as lonely an end as that of the compulsive bassoon player.

A writer's problem does not change. It is always how to write truly and having found out what is true to project it in such a way that it becomes part of the experience of the person who reads it.

There is no rule on how to write. Sometimes it comes easily and perfectly; sometimes it's like drilling rock and then blasting it out with charges.

Cowardice, as distinguished from panic, is almost always simply a lack of ability to suspend the functioning of the imagination.

There are events which are so great that if a writer has participated in them, his obligation is to write truly rather than assume the presumption of altering them with invention.

A man's got to take a lot of punishment to write a really funny book.

It's enough for you to do it once for a few men to remember you. But if you do it year after year, then many people remember you and they tell it to their children, and their children and grandchildren remember and, if it concerns books, they can read them. And if it's good enough, it will last as long as there are human beings.

Opposite: Luxembourg Museum.

Above: In his study in the White Tower, Cuba, 1952. Opposite: Front-page review, New York Times.

You know lots of criticism is written by characters who are very academic and think it is a sign you are worthless if you make jokes or kid or even clown. I wouldn't kid Our Lord if he was on the cross. But I would attempt a joke with him if I ran into him chasing the money changers out of the temple.

It doesn't matter that I don't write for a day or a year or ten years as long as the knowledge that I *can* write is solid inside me. But a day without that knowledge, or not being sure of it, is eternity.

> All my life I've looked at words as though I were seeing them for the first time.

THE NEW NOVEL BY HEMINGWAY

"For Whom the Bell Tolls" Is the Best Book He Has Written

FOR WHOM THE BELL TOLLS. By Ernest Hemingway. 471 pp. New York: Charles Scribner's Sons. $2.75.

By J. DONALD ADAMS

THIS is the best book Ernest Hemingway has written, the fullest, the deepest, the truest. It will, I think, be one of the major novels in American literature.

There were those of us who felt, when "To Have and Have Not" was published, that Hemingway was through as a creative writer. That is always a dangerous assumption to make regarding any writer of much innate ability, but it did seem that Hemingway was blocked off from further development. We were badly mistaken. Technical skill he had long ago acquired; the doubt lay in where and how he could apply it, and that doubt he has now sweepingly erased. The skill is even further sharpened than it was, but with it has come an inner growth, a deeper and surer feeling for life, than he has previously displayed. Whatever brought about this growth—whether his experience of the Spanish war, out of which this novel was made, or something else, it is plainly to be seen in this book, from beginning to end. There are no traces of adolescence in the Hemingway of "For Whom the Bell Tolls." This is the work of a mature artist, of a mature mind.

The title derives from John Donne. The passage from which it comes faces the book's first page:

No man is an Iland, intire of it selfe; every man is a peece of the Continent, a part of the maine; if a Clod bee washed away by the Sea, Europe is the lesse, as well as if a Promontorie were, as well as if a Mannor of thy friends or of thine owne were; any mans death diminishes me, because I am involved in Mankinde; And therefore never send to know for whom the bell tolls; it tolls for thee.

It is a fine title, and an apt one, for this is a book filled with the imminence of death, and the manner of man's meeting it. That is as it should be; this is a story of the Spanish war. But in it Hemingway has struck universal chords, and he has struck them vibrantly. Perhaps it conveys something of the measure of "For Whom the Bell Tolls" to say that with that theme, it is not a depressing but an uplifting book. It has the purging quality that lies in the presenting of tragic but profound truth. Hemingway has freed himself from the negation that held him in his other novels. As Robert Jordan lay facing death he looked down the hill slope and thought: "I have fought for what I believed in for a year now. If we win here we win everywhere. The world is a fine place and worth the fighting

for and I hate very much to leave it."

The frame of the story is a minor incident in the horror that was the war in Spain. Robert Jordan is a young American in the Loyalist ranks who has been detailed to the blowing up of a bridge which the General Staff wants destroyed

Ernest Hemingway.

to prevent the bringing up of enemy reinforcements. His mission carried him into hill country where he must seek the aid of guerrilla bands. Jordan destroys the bridge, but while he is escaping with his companions his horse is knocked from under him by an exploding shell, and we leave him lying on the hillside, his leg crushed by the animal's fall. He sends his companions on and waits, with a submachine gun beside him, for the enemy's approach.

Those who leave him are, with Jordan,

the main figures in the story. Among them is the girl Maria, whom Jordan, in the four-day span of the story's action, has met and loved. And as "For Whom the Bell Tolls" is a better story of action than "A Farewell to Arms," so too is this a finer love story than that of Lieutenant Henry and Catherine Barkley. That is saying a good deal, but it is true. I know of no love scenes in American fiction few to any other to compare with those of "For Whom the Bell Tolls" in depth and sincerity of feeling. They are unerringly right, and as much beyond those of "A Farewell to Arms" as the latter were beyond the casual couplings of "The Sun Also Rises."

The book holds, I think, the best character drawing that Hemingway has done. Robert Jordan is a fine portrait of a fighting idealist, and the Spanish figures are superbly done, in particular the woman Pilar, who should take her place among the memorable women of fiction—earthy and strong, tender, hard, wise, a woman who, as she said of herself, would have been a good man, and yet was a woman made for men. The brutal, unstable Pablo, in whom strength and evil were combined, the good and brave old man Anselmo—these and others are warmly living in this heroic story.

I wrote once that Ernest Hemingway can see and describe with a precision and a vividness unmatched since Kipling first displayed his great visual gift. There are scenes in this book finer than any he has done. The telling of how the Civil Guard was shot in Pablo's town and how the fascists were beaten to death between rows of men armed with flails and hurled over a cliff into the river 300 feet below, how the fascists walked out one by one from their prayers in the City Hall and severally met their deaths, has the thrust and power of one of the more terrible of Goya's pictures.

In all that goes to make a good novel "For Whom the Bell Tolls" is an advance beyond Hemingway's previous work. It is much more full-bodied in its drawing of character, visually more brilliant, and incomparably richer in content. Hemingway's style, too, has changed for the better. It was extraordinarily effective at times before, but it is shed now of the artificialities that clung to it. There is nothing obtrusive about the manner in which this book is written; the style is a part of the whole; there is no artifice to halt the eye. It has simplicity and power, delicacy and strength.

This is Hemingway's longest novel, and it could be, I think, as most books can, a little shorter, and with benefit. It seems to me that some of the long passages in which Robert Jordan's mind turns back to his days in Madrid retard the narrative unnecessarily and could well have been omitted. If there are other flaws in this fine performance, I have not yet found them. A very good novel it unquestionably is, and I am not at all sure that it may not prove to be a great one. That is not something to determine on a first reading. But this much more is certain: that Hemingway is now a writer of real stature, not merely a writer of abundant talent whose work does not measure up to his equipment. "For Whom the Bell Tolls" is the book of a man who knows what life is about, and who can convey his knowledge. Hemingway has found bigger game than the kudu and the lion. The hunter is home from the hill.

All my life I had been struggling to perfect my ear to record exactly what I heard, and I was a sad son of a bitch when I discovered they had invented a machine that put all my training out of business.

⁂

You go against the grain, you're bound to get splinters, but that's the price of not conforming. The risk of originality is humiliation which is another way of saying failure. In high school I once wrote an essay entirely in dialogue and I got an F, not because the dialogue was inferior, but because no one had ever written an essay like that before. "Essays," the teacher said, "are proper sentences, not dialogue." Form over content. When I first set out from home, the report card of my life wasn't very good, but then my grades gradually improved, the more I convinced 'em that finding my own way, on the road and on the page, had its merits.

⁂

I still need more healthy rest in order to work at my best. My health is the main capital I have, and I want to administer it intelligently.

⁂

For a long time now I have tried simply to write the best I can. Sometimes I have good luck and write better than I can.

⁂

Writing and travel broaden your ass if not your mind, so I like to write standing up.

⁂

My aim is to put down on paper what I see and what I feel in the best and simplest way.

Opposite: El Escorial, Spain, the setting of For Whom the Bell Tolls.

⁂

The racing form is the true art of fiction.

If you're going to be a writer, sooner or later you write about everything—the places you went—the people who double-crossed you—how the weather was—the ladies you fucked—your wins and your losses—and those funny times when you mistakenly thought the world was made for you.

Decadence is a difficult word to use since it has become little more than a term of abuse applied by critics to anything they do not yet understand or which seems to differ from their moral concepts.

Opposite: Churriana, Spain, 1958.

God knows people who are paid to have attitudes toward things, professional critics, make me sick; camp-following eunuchs of literature. They won't even whore. They're all virtuous and sterile. And how well meaning and high minded. But they're all camp followers.

The most essential gift for a good writer is a built-in, shock-proof, shit detector. This is the writer's radar, and all great writers have had it.

The only truly good novel, maybe great, to come out of World War II is *The Gallery*. I say "maybe great" because who in the hell can tell? Greatness is the longest marathon ever run; many enter; few survive.

You have to repeat yourself again and again as a man but you should not do so as a writer.

The writer must have a devotion to his work that a priest of God has for his.

Black Dog is mostly a springer spaniel who wandered into our Sun Valley ski cabin one afternoon, cold, starved, fear ridden and sub-dog in complex—a hunting dog who was scared stiff of gunfire. I brought him back to Cuba and patiently and lovingly built up his weight, confidence, and affection to the point that Black Dog believed he was an accomplished author himself. He needs ten hours' sleep but is always exhausted because he faithfully follows my schedule. When I'm between books he is happy, but when I'm working he takes it very hard. Although he's a boy who loves his sleep, he thinks he has to get up and stick with me from first light on. He keeps his eyes open loyally. But he doesn't like it.

With Mary, his fourth wife, and Black Dog at Finca Vigía, Cuba, 1948.

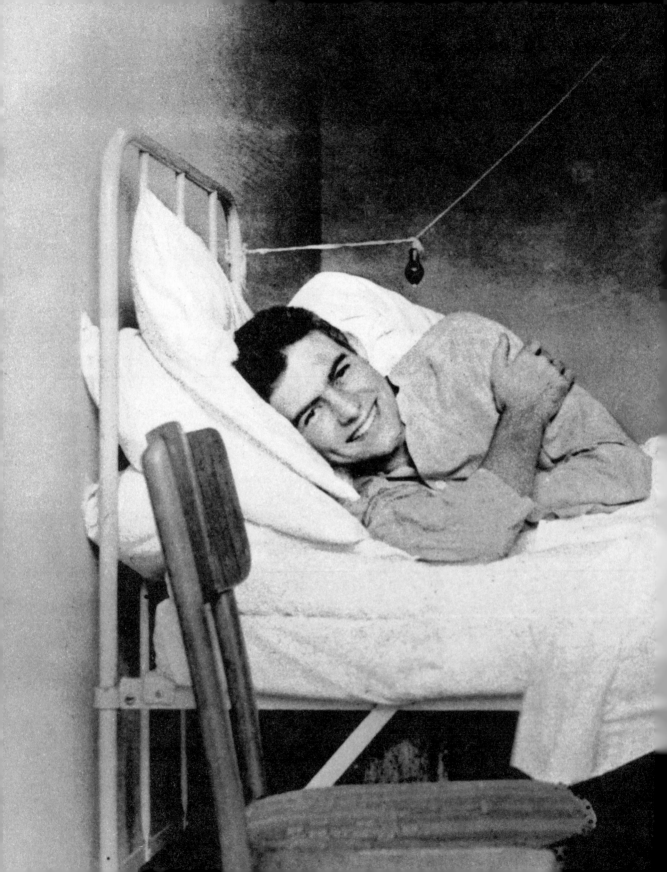

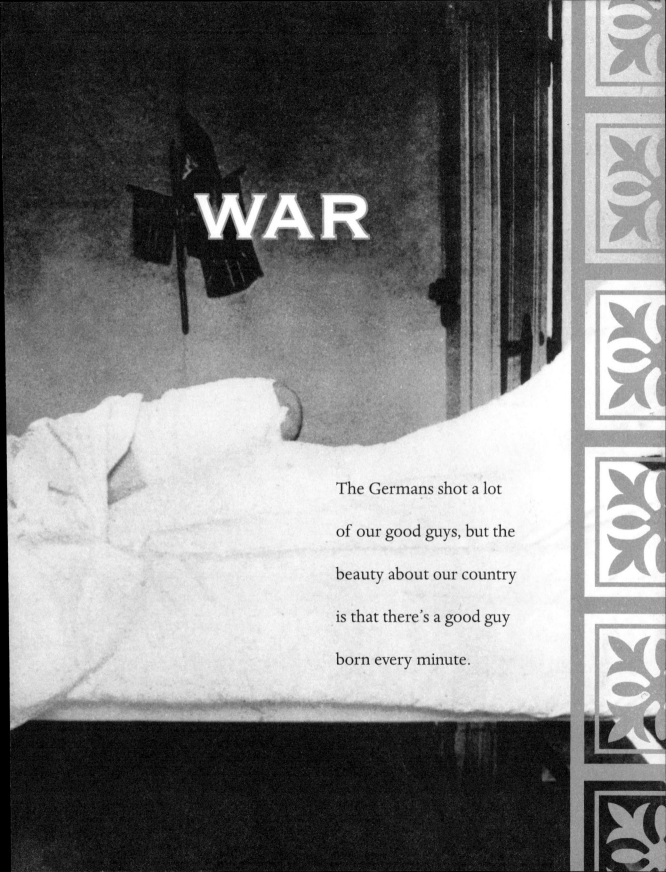

WAR

The Germans shot a lot
of our good guys, but the
beauty about our country
is that there's a good guy
born every minute.

Never think that war, no matter how necessary, nor how justified, is not a crime.

I used to keep a bowl by the side of my bed, full of the metal fragments they took from my leg, and people used to come and take them as good-luck souvenirs. Two hundred twenty-seven pieces. Right leg. True count. Got hit with a Minenwerfer that had been lobbed in by an Austrian trench mortar. They would fill these Minenwerfers with the goddamnedest collection of crap you ever saw—nuts, bolts, screws, nails, spikes, metal scrap—and when they blew, you caught whatever you were in the way of. Three Italians with me had their legs blown off. I was lucky. The kneecap was down on my shin and the leg had caught all that metal, but the kneecap was still attached. The big fight was to keep them from sawing off the leg. They awarded me the Croce al Merito di Guerra with three citations, and the Medaglia d'Argento al Valore Militare. I threw them into the bowl with the other scrap metal.

The wound combat makes in you, as a writer, is a very slow-healing one.

Previous page: In a Milan hospital, World War I, his leg seriously injured. Opposite: World War I, Italian army, before being injured.

There is a military cliché: Better to die on your feet than to live on your knees, but you better get on your belly damn fast if you want to stay alive in plenty places.

I believe that all the people who stand to profit by a war and who help provoke it should be shot on the first day it starts by accredited representatives of the loyal citizens of their country who will fight it.

When the moment to fight arrives, whether it is in a barroom or in a war, the thing to do is to hit your opponent the first punch and hit him as hard as possible. But we were a great and noble power, and the Japanese relied on our nobility and kept men talking to us while they prepared to hit.

When working with irregular troops, you have no real discipline except that of example. As long as they believe in you, they will fight, if they are good elements. The minute they cease to believe in you or in the mission to be accomplished, they disappear.

Opposite: At Milan's San Siro racetrack, with his love, Agnes Von Kurowsky, at his right. Below: Ernest on crutches, convalescing at a Red Cross hospital in Milan.

The wars
ruined my
sleep—that
and my
goddamn
thin eyelids.

During the war, what I had for a lucky piece was a red stone
my son Bumby had given me, but one morning in England when
I was scheduled to fly a mission with the RAF, the floor maid
at my hotel brought back my pants from the cleaners and I
realized that I had left the stone in one of the pockets and the
cleaner had thrown it away. The RAF car was already waiting for
me downstairs to go to the airfield, and I was really sweating over
hitting a mission to Germany without the lucky piece. So I said
to the maid, "Give me something for a lucky piece—just anything
and wish me luck on it and that will do it." Well, she didn't have
anything in the pocket of her uniform but she picked up the cork
from a bottle of Mumm I had drunk the night before and gave me
that. Damn good thing I had it—every plane on that flight
got chewed up except ours.

Never mistake motion for action.

I have been shot at two years longer than General Grant.

General Modesto of our Republican army was in love with Miss Martha, my third wife, made three passes at her in my presence, so I invited him to step into the men's can. All right, General, I said, let's have it out. We hold handkerchiefs in our mouths and keep firing till one of us drops. We got out our handkerchiefs and our guns, but a pal of mine came in and talked me out of it because money was scarce and our side could not afford a monument, which all deceased Spanish generals get automatically.

Opposite: Martha Gellhorn, Ernest's third wife, hunting pheasants, Ketchum, Idaho. Above: With General Buck Lanham, Battle of the Bulge, World War II. Left: Sightseeing in Milan during his convalescence.

Once we have a war there is only one thing to do.
It must be won. For defeat brings worse things than
any that can ever happen in war.

Why the hell do the good and the brave have to die
before everyone else?

*Below: RAF bomb
mission, World
War II, 1944. Oppo-
site: Entertaining
Air Force personnel
at Finca Vigía.*

In modern war you will die like a dog for no good reason.

Courage is grace under pressure.

In deep-sea fishing, watch the boat

vibration. If you can hear it, then the

fish can hear it and won't come up.

That's the only trick.

SPORTS

Regarding sports, I was a mediocre ballplayer, a slightly better football player, a worthless tennis player, and a contemptible performer on the violoncello and tuba. Boxing I learned the really hard way, and I had a certain aptitude for it. Anything about boxing or fighting is my own business and I could always be broke and wish to write about it myself. I deplore the tendency that any literate man should have everything that he knows about and has personally experienced written about by someone else who neither knows about it nor has experienced it. This is especially true about fishing and shooting, which were the only things I was ever good at. These are sports which are not performed in public nor in stadiums, and so those who are any good at them, if they tell about them truly are almost invariably regarded as liars.

Previous page: At the age of five, Ernest was already an accomplished fisherman on the northern Michigan lakes. Right: Ernest, second row on the right, with the Oak Park High School football team. Following pages: Gstaad, Switzerland, 1927; and skiing at Schruns in the Austrian Alps, 1926 (inset).

Now the field of big-game hunting especially has become the province of the professional liar. There are even entire magazines devoted to the exploits of these dubious characters. A man who has done anything worth doing should keep his mouth shut, and if he writes, write only for those who know what he is writing about. Auto racing, bullfighting, and mountain climbing are the only real sports . . . all others are games.

Following page:
Captions to come.

The professors in their thin, erudite volumes describe my unhappy childhood, which supposedly motivated all my literary drives. Christ, I never had an unhappy day I can remember! I was no good at football, but does that make an unhappy boyhood? Zuppke put me at center, but I never knew what a digit was—I skipped third grade so never found out about digits—so I couldn't figure out the plays. I used to look at my teammates' faces and guess who looked like they expected the ball. I was called Drag-Ass when they put me at guard. I wanted to play backfield but they knew better. There was one guy on the team beat me up in the locker room every day for two years, but then I grew up to him and I beat the be-Jesus out of him and that was the end of that.

One thing about big upsets in the boxing ring—the odds-on favorite who just couldn't get going—Don't ask him if he ate himself out of the title or drank himself out of it or trained himself stale—just ask him if he got laid the night before.

Skiing now, with the lifts and all, is about like roller skating. Nobody has any strength in their legs because they never climb anymore, and the best concession around a ski joint is the X-ray and plaster-cast booth.

Of those who criticize
cockfighting as cruel may
I ask: What else does a
fighting cock like to do?

You can tell if a horse is fixed by his eyes, his nostrils, and his black sweat.

If you fight a great left-hooker, sooner or later he will knock you on your ass. He will get the left where you can't see it, and in it comes like a brick. Life is the greatest left-hooker so far, although many say it was Jack Britton. Jack kept on his toes and moved around and never let them hit him solid. When he fought the great Benny Leonard, Jack was asked how he beat Benny so easily. Well, I'll tell you, Jack said. This Benny was an awfully smart boxer. All the time he's boxing, he's thinking. And all the time he was thinking, I was hitting him.

Opposite: Training his fighting cocks, Finca Vigía. Below: With Ringling Brothers circus horses, Cuba.

I agree with Sam Langford, who said that fighters could sweat out eating too much and could sweat out beer and whiskey, but nobody could sweat out women. Fighters' legs go from women; ballplayers from the sudden stops.

One of the things I liked best in life was to wake early in the morning with the birds singing and the windows open and the sound of horses jumping. When I was young in Paris, I was the only outsider who was allowed into the private training grounds at Achères. That's how I came to know about Epinard. A trainer named J. Patrick, an expatriate American who had been a friend of mine since the time we were both kids in the Italian army, told me that Gene Leigh had a colt that might be the horse of the century. Those were Patrick's words, "the horse of the century." He said, "Ernie, take my advice—beg, borrow, or steal all the cash you can get your hands on and get it down on this two-year-old for the first start. After that there'll never be odds again. But that first start, before they know that name, get down on him."

It was my complete poverty period—I didn't even have milk money for Bumby, but I followed Patrick's advice. I hit everyone for cash. I even borrowed a thousand francs from my barber. I accosted strangers. There wasn't a sou in Paris that hadn't been nailed down that I didn't solicit; so I was really "on" Epinard when he started in the Prix Yacoulef at Deauville for his debut. His price was fifty-nine to ten. He won in a breeze, and I was able to support myself for six or eight months on the winnings. I had learned something valuable—always trust reliable sources.

The old Enghien was my all-time-favorite track. It had a relaxed, unbuttoned atmosphere. One of the last times I went there was with Evan Shipman, who was a professional handicapper as well as a writer, and Harold Stearns, who was "Peter Pickum" for the Paris edition of the *Chicago Tribune* at the time—Harold and Evan were relying on form and drew a blank on the day's card. I hit six winners out of eight. Harold was rather testy about my wins and asked me for the secret of my success. "It was easy," I told him. "I went down to the paddock between races, and I smelled them. The truth is, where horses are concerned, the nose will triumph over science and reason every time."

I wish I still had my nose, but I can't trust it anymore. I can trace the decline of my infallible-nose period to the day John Dos Passos and I came out to the track to make our winter stake. We were both working on books and we needed enough cash to get us through the winter. I had touted Dos onto my paddock sniffing as a sure thing, and we had pooled everything we had. One of the horses in the seventh race smelled especially good to me, so we put our whole stake on him. He fell at the first jump. We didn't have a sou in our pockets and we had to walk all the way back to the Left Bank from here.

Opposite: Sparring with a native while on safari. Below: Steeplechasing at Enghien.

When you attend every day of a fall steeplechase meet at Auteuil—
the emerald racetrack in the heart of the Bois de Boulogne—you
get a wonderful rhythm, like playing ball every day, and you get to
know the track, so they can't fool you. There's a beauty restaurant
at the top, hung right over the track, where you can eat good and
watch them as though you were riding in the race. They bring you
the *côte jaune* with the changing odds three times for each race, and
you can bet right there, no rushing up and down to the bet cages
with your unsettled food jiggling. It's too easy, but wonderful for
scouting a race.

We were staying at the Ritz when I got a call at six in the morning
from the jockey room at Auteuil, mentioning a mount named Bataclan in the seventh steeplechase race on that day's card, with odds
at twenty-seven to one. We rustled up a large bundle of francs to
put on Bataclan's nose, but when we went down to the paddock to
study our horse and the other horses as they paraded by, I thought

*Above: The old track,
Enghien.*

that two other horses in the race had superior smells, Klipper and Killibi. At the start, Bataclan took the lead, then faded to second on the upgraded backstretch, lost more ground on the water jump, and on the turn it was Killibi, Klipper, and Bataclan in that order, with Bataclan twenty lengths off the pace. But as Killibi took the last hedge, pressed by Klipper, his jockey reached for the bat, and in so doing loosened his grip; Killibi's front legs dropped slightly and scraped the hedge, breaking his stride, causing him to stumble and pitch forward, with his rider jumping clear. Klipper's jockey tried to clear the fallen Killibi but he couldn't, and Klipper went down right on top of Killibi, the jock hitting the turf hard and not moving.

Bataclan's jockey had plenty of time to see what had happened, so he veered Bataclan to the other side of the hedge and came in five lengths to the good. We returned to the Ritz with a Matterhorn of ten-thousand-franc notes, which, coming as they did on December 21, were plowed back into France's Christmas economy. Packages covered both beds and spilled onto the floor. Never had so few bought so much, but happily, not one thing anybody gave to anybody was useful.

And it reinforced my mantra that one should never doubt the honesty of a jockey-room tip.

Down here in Cuba, if you are over forty, you can have a boy run for you and still stay in the baseball game. In our family my youngest boy, Gigi, used to try to knock everybody's cap off on the first pitch. He did it to me, too, in a pickup game, and I walked out to him, having got up from the dirt—the older you get, by the way, the slower you can hit the dirt—and I said, "Don't you know any better than to throw at your own father?" But all it occurs to him to say, looking at me as mean as a warthog, is, "Don't you know there aren't any fathers on a ball field?"

Sun is the best bullfighter. When the day is overcast, it is like a stage show without lights. The matador's worst enemy is wind.

There are only three things to bullfighting—*parar*, to keep the feet quiet; *templar*, to move the cloth slowly; *mandar*, to dominate and control the animal by the cloth. When you watch a matador, look only for these things, do not be fooled by the circusing.

Why is it good bullfighters have all the good bulls?

Above, left to right: Matador Ordóñez, Madrid, 1959; Matador Calerito, Valencia, 1959; Matador Domínguin, Valencia, 1959; Matador Pedrés, 1959; Matador Ortega, Madrid, 1959; Matador Domínguin, tienta, 1959.

There are bullfighters who do it just for the money—they are worthless. The only one who matters is the bullfighter who feels it, so that if he did it for nothing, he would do it as well. Same holds true for damn near everyone else.

Bullfighting is the only art in which the artist is in danger of death, and in which the degree of brilliance in the performance is left to the fighter's honor.

I long ago resolved never to be friends with a matador again, because the agony for me was too great on those days when my friends could not handle the bull because of fear. On any given day, any matador, no matter how great or how young, can suffer an attack of fear and be virtually incapacitated. When it used to hit my friends I suffered right along with them, but it was an idiotic torture, since I was not hired for the job and its agonies. So I swore off matadors as friends.

The daylight between a matador's groin and the bull's passing horns increases as his wealth increases.

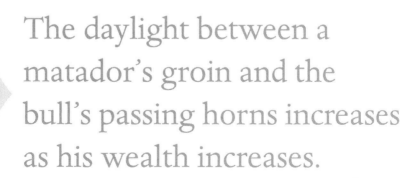

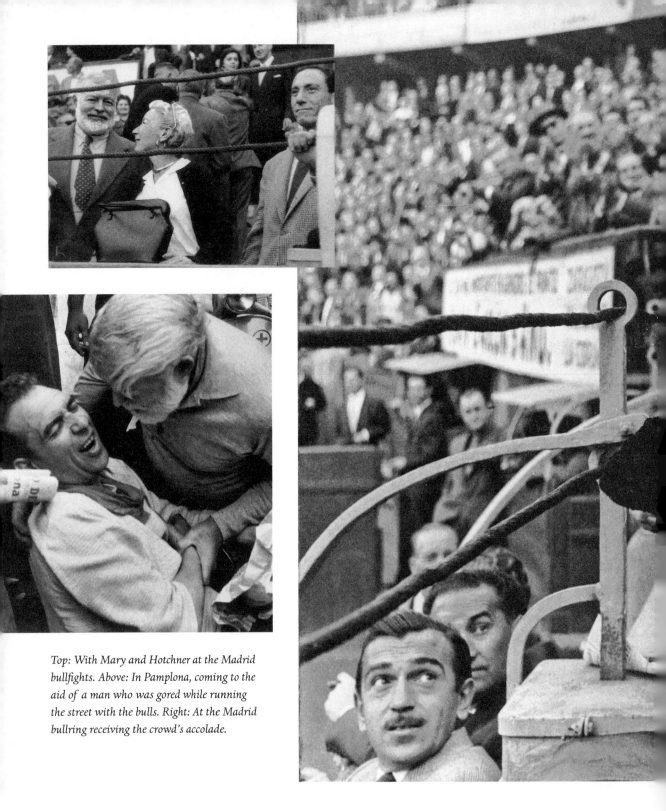

Top: With Mary and Hotchner at the Madrid bullfights. Above: In Pamplona, coming to the aid of a man who was gored while running the street with the bulls. Right: At the Madrid bullring receiving the crowd's accolade.

U Undeclared homosexuals follow bullfighters.

About moral, I know only that what is moral is what you feel good after and what is immoral is what you feel bad after, and judged by these moral standards, which I do not defend, the bullfight is very moral to me, because I feel very fine while it is going on and have a feeling of life and death and mortality and immortality, and after it is over I feel very sad but very fine.

Fighting a big fish, fast and unaided, never resting, nor letting the fish rest, is comparable to a ten-round fight in the ring in its requirements for good physical condition. Most honest and skillful anglers who lose big fish do so because the fish whips them, and they cannot hold him when he decides, toward the end of the fight, to sound and, sounding, dies.

Opposite: Fighting bulls entering the Pamplona ring. Below: Fishing, Cojímar.

Right: Battling a marlin. Below: The Pilar
*off Veradero Beach, Cuba, Ernest topside.
Opposite: Castro's fishing tournament.*

As a fisherman, Castro could not win his own fishing tournament, even though it was rigged.

HOLLYWOOD

If you ask me, Gary Cooper and

Ingrid Bergman were superstars

both on and off the screen.

You see the cinema version? [*For Whom the Bell Tolls*] The big love scene between Coops and Ingrid and he didn't take off his coat. That's one hell of a way for a guy to make love, with his coat on—in a sleeping bag. And Ingrid, in her tailored dress and all those pretty curls—she was strictly Elizabeth Arden out of Abercrombie and Fitch.

Previous page: With Gary Cooper and Ingrid Bergman, Sun Valley, Idaho, 1948. Above: With Jane Russell, Ketchum, Idaho. Opposite: with Marlene Dietrich.

I saw the movie they made of *The Sun Also Rises*, the day before the start of the 1957 World Series, for which I had made a special trip to New York. All I can say is, any picture in which Errol Flynn is the best actor is its own worst enemy.

A very excited operator's voice told me that Darryl F. Zanuck himself of Twentieth Century-Fox was going to speak to me. And by golly he did! "Hello, Ernest?" he said (you could tell it was Hollywood, because here he was calling me Ernest, and we only knew each other from having exchanged my story for his dough). "Ernest, we are in executive session here in my conference room, and we've been wrestling all day with a crisis that only you can resolve. We have made a truly wonderful picture of your wonderful story 'The Short Happy Life of Francis Macomber,' and we're ready for distribution, but we feel that the title is too long for the average movie marquee, so we would appreciate it very much if you could change it to something short, with eye appeal—you know, a title that would create on-sight excitement—something that'll appeal to both sexes and make them feel they have to see the movie." I told Zanuck to hold on while I gave the matter some thought. The bartender mixed me a drink and every once in a while I'd go back to the phone to tell the operator not to cut us off because I was engaged in emergency thinking. Finally, when I felt my A.T. and T. stock had gone up a couple of points, I said that I thought I had just what the doctor ordered. Zanuck said he had his pencil at the ready. Now, I said, you want something short and exciting that will catch the eye of both sexes, right? Well, then, here it is: F as in Fox, U as in Universal, C as in Culver City and K as in R.K.O. That should fit all the marquees, and you can't beat it as a sex symbol.

Following page:
With Lauren Bacall.

I read about the movie version of *The Snows of Kilimanjaro* and how there was only one minor alteration—the man is rescued and lives instead of dying—a very minor change, don't you think?

The only two I could sit through were *The Killers* and *To Have and Have Not*— I guess Ava Gardner and Lauren Bacall had a lot to do with it.

Hollywood may magnanimously offer the writer what they vaguely call "a piece of the picture" but the only words that have any meaning are: "No, thanks, I want the cash up front."

I received a telegram from the producer David O. Selznick, who had just completed a remake of *A Farewell to Arms* with his wife, Jennifer Jones, starring as the novel's heroine, Catherine Barkley. Selznick had not paid me anything for this version, because back in the twenties the book had been sold outright, with no provision for remakes. This telegram said that Selznick had just informed the world press that, although not legally obligated to, he was hereby pledging himself to pay Mr. Hemingway $50,000 from the profits of the picture, if and when it earned any profits. I sent Mr. Selznick a telegram in reply saying that if by some miracle, your movie, which stars forty-one-year-old Mrs. Selznick portraying twenty-four-year-old Catherine Barkley, does earn $50,000, you should have all $50,000 changed into nickels at your local bank and shove them up your ass until they came out of your ears. You know, you write a book like that that you're fond of over the years, then you see that happen to it, it's like pissing in your father's beer.

Opposite: With Myrna Loy and William Powell. Above: Rock Hudson with the director of the remake of A Farewell to Arms. *Left: A marlin Ernest landed for the movie of* Old Man and the Sea.

The only movie that I had anything to do with was *The Old Man and the Sea*. I edited the script and then spent weeks with a camera crew off the coast of Peru, catching large marlins that never got hooked at the right hour for the Technicolor cameras; so like all movie marlins, they wound up being sponge-rubber fish in a Culver City tank. I sat through all of that movie, numb. Spencer Tracy looked like a fat, very rich actor playing a fisherman.

In shooting you've got

to be careful, not worried.

HUNTING

Best training I got for shooting birds was from my father. He used to give me only three shells for a whole day's hunting, and he was very strict about shooting only on the wing. He had his spies around, so I never tried to cheat.

❖

Shoot lions at one hundred yards because a lion can cover one hundred yards in three and three-fourths seconds. You've got to break bone. If you just shoot a lion, it won't stop him. You've got to shoot like a surgeon to break bone. And watch for the lioness. While you are posing with one foot up on her dead husband she will sail in and tear you in half. That makes a rather messy photo for the folks back home.

To shoot good, you've got to get calm first, calm inside, as if you're in a church and you've got something to believe in—then let go.

Previous pages: Hailey, Idaho, 1950. Opposite: Duck shoot, Venice, 1948. Left: Early on, Ernest had his very own gun.

Opposite: Shooting a cigarette from the lips of Matador Ordóñez. Top: With Adriana and one of his trophies. Above: With members of the Havana shooting club, Cuba. Left: With Pauline, his second wife; and a trophy lion, Serengeti Plain, 1934.

In New York birds fly, but they are not serious about it. They don't climb.

Had an English friend who wanted to shoot a lion with bow and arrow. One White Hunter after another turned him down until finally a Swede White Hunter agreed to take him. Englishman was the kind of Englishman who took a portable bar on safari. Swede, who was a very good hunter, warned against the bow and arrow as effective, but His Lordship insisted. They finally stalk the lion, set it up, lion charges, Englishman pulls back bow, hits lion in the chest at fifty yards, lion bites off the arrow, keeps coming, eats the ass right off one of the native guides in one gulping tear before Swede can drop him. Englishman is shook up. Comes over to look at the bloody mess of native guide and lion lying side by side. Swede says, "Well, Your Lordship, you may now put the bow and arrow away." Englishman says, "I think we might."

There was this very big, cocky black bear out west who had made life miserable for everyone by standing in the middle of the road and refusing to budge when cars came along. It got so that no one could use the road. I heard about him and drove along the road to seek him out; suddenly, sure enough—there was the bear. A really big bear. He was on his hind legs and his upper lip was pulled back in a sneer. I got out of the car and went over to him. "Do you realize that you're nothing but a miserable, common black bear?" I said to him in a loud, firm voice. "Why, you sad son of a bitch, how can you be so cocky and stand there and block cars when you're nothing but a miserable bear and a black bear at that—not even a polar or a grizzly or anything worthwhile." I really laid it on him, and the poor black bear began to hang his head, then he lowered himself to all fours and pretty soon he walked off the road. I had destroyed him. From that time on he used to run behind a tree and hide whenever he saw a car coming and shake with fear that I might be inside, ready to dress him down.

Opposite and left: A rhino bagged on safari. Following page: Ketchum, Idaho, 1959.

I love to go to the zoo.
But not on Sunday. I don't
like to see the people
making fun of the animals,
when it should be the
other way around.

There was this easterner who came to me one day and asked me to help him shoot a grizzly. "It's all my wife wants. Night and day she's after me, and since we were just married, I'd like to please her." Hell, I say, the grizzly is the hardest of all bears to shoot, the toughest and the smartest. I haven't shot a grizzly in eight years. Well, I am out with this husband and wife one day, and we are stalking a moose for food when there's a sound in the brush and three grizzlies uncover. They are gargantuan sons of bitches. I tell the wife to get behind me because we have no time to try to get to cover. The husband, who is some distance away, has already covered and is out of the action. Now, a grizzly will drop when hit right, but he will usually recover and charge and won't drop again until he's dead. That's what makes them so damn dangerous. The nearest grizzly, an eight-hundred-pounder, takes one look at us and charges straight on. I drop him with a neck shot and then, as he starts the get-up, I drill him in the shoulder for keeps. The second grizzly charges as I am reloading, and I empty both shells into him practically point-blank. He is dead on arrival. Now the third grizzly, who has cased the fate of his buddies and wants no part of it, turns and starts up the hill, and I have to peg him four times before I put him away for good. The new wife emerges from the shadow of my behind and she says to me, "My mouth is dry. Please cover me while I go to the stream to get a drink." That's all she ever says about the whole episode. And they want to know if Margot Macomber was drawn from real life!

Opposite: Learning about spears and arrows from the Masai. Above: Posing with his Wyoming grizzlies, 1932.

EXPLORING

Italians are wonderful people.

Probably have had the worst

press in the world.

I once had a room at the St. James et Albany in Paris, and at the bottom of the porcelain toilet bowl there was a pair of blue lovebirds. Made me constipated.

I always feel wonderful here [Escorial, Spain]. Like I've gone to heaven under the best auspices. Very hard to worry under these conditions. Also feel very secure because of local motto: "A man with a beard will never starve."

Have you noticed that toothless people the world over, regardless of language, sound the same?

I love Africa and I feel it's another home, and anytime a man can feel that, not counting where he's born, is where he's meant to be.

I like heat, but it can really get too hot in St. Louis, Senegal, Bilbao, and Madrid.

In Zurich they overbell you to death.

Previous pages: Hemingway's favorite Venetian scene, as he saw it from his balcony at the Gritti Palace Hotel. Opposite: En route from Aigues-Mortes to Nîmes, with driver, Adamo. Above: With friends in Tanganyika, 1934.

When in Paris, the only thing one should leave to chance is the Loterie Nationale.

Why live in New York or London when there's Venice and Paris?

I found that learning all the Romance languages was made easier by reading the newspapers—an English-language paper in the morning and then the foreign-language paper in the afternoon—it was the same news and the familiarity with the news events helped me understand the afternoon papers.

On our last trip [Africa] I had a tick on my prick for four days. All local remedies, such as burning the tick's ass and rubbing lion dung on him, failed. Even tried a pair of tweezers. Finally Philip Percival, our White Hunter, suggested suffocating him in candle wax. We dripped a mound of candle wax on him, and sure enough, it worked. That's one remedy you won't find in *Black's Medical Dictionary*.

Switzerland is a small, steep country, much more up and down than sideways, and is all stuck over with large brown hotels built in the cuckoo style of architecture.

Right: Zaragoza, Spain. Opposite: With an accommodating circus elephant, Cuba. Opposite (inset): With buffalo, Serengeti Plain, 1934.

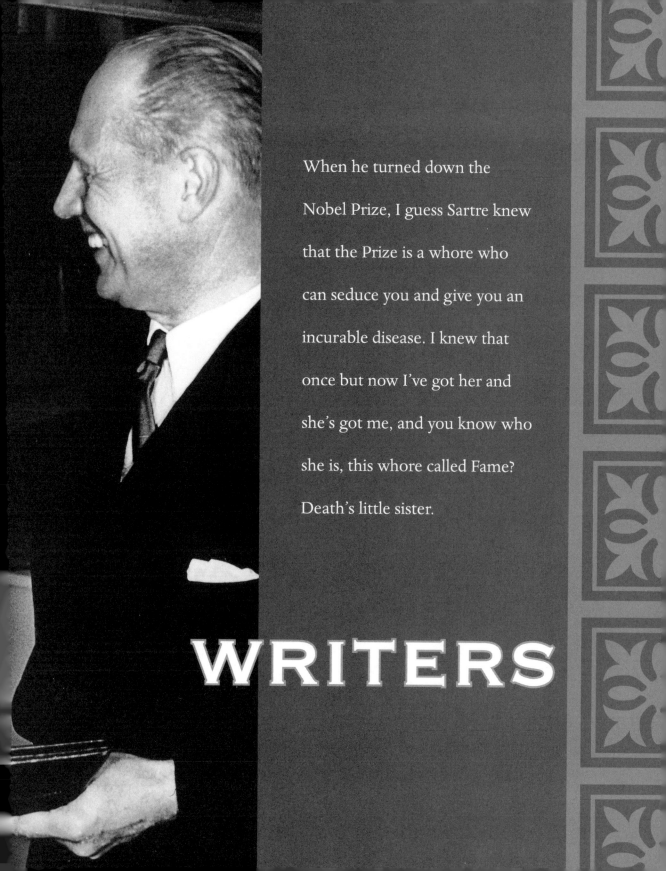

When he turned down the Nobel Prize, I guess Sartre knew that the Prize is a whore who can seduce you and give you an incurable disease. I knew that once but now I've got her and she's got me, and you know who she is, this whore called Fame? Death's little sister.

WRITERS

Sartre told me at dinner last night that a newspaperman made up the word *existentialism* and that he, Sartre, had nothing to do with it.

Gertrude Stein once said that Scott's flame and my flame weren't the same. Scott was so damn insecure he decided she meant I had a bigger or brighter flame than he did. When he first brought it up, I said all the talk about flames was Stein horseshit, since we were both serious writers who would write the best we could until we died and there was no competition between flames or anything else. But he kept on. And on, and on.

Previous pages: The Swedish ambassador presents Hemingway with the Nobel Prize for Literature, Cuba, 1954. Right: Gertrude Stein and Alice Toklas. Opposite: Leicester Hemingway.

Sometimes I wish I had a ghost writer. By Ernest Hemingway as told to Truman Capote.

Gertrude Stein was a complainer. So she labeled that generation with her complaint. But it was bullshit. There was no movement, no tight band of pot-smoking nihilists wandering around looking for Mommy to lead them out of the dada wilderness. What there was, was a lot of people around the same age who had been through the war and now were writing or composing or whatever, and other people who had not been through the war and either wished they had been or wished they were writing or boasted about not being in the war. Nobody I knew at that time thought of himself as wearing the silks of the Lost Generation, or had even heard the label. We were a pretty solid mob. The characters in *The Sun Also Rises* were tragic, but the real hero was the earth, and you get the sense of its triumph in abiding forever.

My brother Leicester has written a book about me that, among other things, contains some of my letters, and he wanted permission to print them. I wrote him my general attitude toward books about people who are still alive, and especially one member of a family writing about that family, especially one as vulnerable as ours, where my mother was a bitch and my father a suicide. I am damned if I will permit Leicester to write about it and dredge up all the trouble I've ever been in as well, just to make money. It might be better to buy the whole thing from him and get a release, but as I explained to him, no Hemingstein has ever yet paid for anything he could prevent with his own two hands.

I've always had the problem of other writers pinching my stuff. During World War II, I traveled around quite a bit with a writer I had known for a long time. I talked things out with him, the way you would with a friend. One day over drinks I told him how I had figured out that the best air-raid alarm was the attitude of cattle in the field. "I can watch a herd of cows," I told him, "and tell you long before you hear any sounds that planes are approaching. The cattle stiffen; they stop grazing. They know." A couple of days later I saw other correspondents congratulating my writer friend I had told about the cattle. I asked what it was all about. "He wrote a wonderful dispatch for his paper on how cattle react to planes," one guy told me. I investigated and found that my pal had been picking my brain for some time and writing a series of articles based on information I had intended using in my own dispatches. "Listen, you bastard," I said to this writer, "if you steal another thing from me, I'll kill you." Two days later he switched to the Pacific theater of operations.

What does you harm as a writer is when other writers steal your stuff. There was a "name" writer who used to steal my stories as fast as I could write them. He'd change the names of the characters and the locale and sell them for more than I got. But I finally found a way to stop him. I stopped writing for two years and the son of a bitch starved to death.

Poor Faulkner. Does he really think big emotions come from big words? He thinks I don't know the ten-dollar words. I know them, all right. But there are older and simpler and better words, and these are the ones I use.

The parody is the last refuge of the frustrated writer. Parodies are what you write when you are associate editor of the *Harvard Lampoon*. The greater the work of literature, the easier the parody. The step up from writing parodies is writing on the wall above the urinal.

I told Scott that being a rummy made him very vulnerable—I mean, a rummy married to a crazy is not the kind of pari-mutuel that aids a writer. I told Scott that because I thought the brutal truth might shake him out of himself, and then I tried to set him up by pointing out that Joyce was as bad a rummy as he was and that most good writers were rummies. How the hell can you bleed over your own personal tragedies when you're a writer? You should welcome them, because serious writers have to be hurt really terrible before they can write seriously. But once you get the hurt and can handle it, consider yourself lucky—that is what there is to write about and you have to be as faithful to it as a scientist is faithful to his laboratory. You can't cheat or pretend. You have to excise the hurt honestly. That's what I told Scott. And I told him that at this point in his life, hurt as he was, he could write twice as well as he ever could, booze or no booze. Zelda or no Zelda. Tried to build him up. Light a fire. Didn't work. He resented my telling him and he was angry and it didn't work at all.

The Nobel Prize be damned! Every day there are letters, phone calls, and brutal interruptions. It is getting on my nerves! I do not want to be driven out of here in the good working months. It is my home and my workplace and I love it. But I am not a public performer, nor am I running for office. I am a writer and I have a right to work and also a right to make a fight to stay alive. Nobody takes the excuse that you want to work or that you've gotten pathological about pieces about you, and one goddamn more and you'd never write another bloody line.

Opposite: William Faulkner. Above: F. Scott Fitzgerald. Following page: James Joyce.

I knew James Joyce from 1921 till his death. In Paris he was always surrounded by professional friends and sycophants. We'd have discussions which would get very heated, and sooner or later Joyce would get in some really rough insult; he was a nice man but nasty, especially if anyone started to talk about writing, nasty as hell, and when he really had everything in an uproar, he would suddenly depart and expect me to handle the characters in his wake who were demanding satisfaction. Joyce was very proud and very rude—especially to jerks. He really enjoyed drinking, and those nights when I'd bring him home after a protracted drinking bout, his wife, Nora, would open the door and say, "Well, here comes James Joyce the author, drunk again with Ernest Hemingway." He was mortally afraid of lightning.

> I'm not going to get into the ring with Tolstoy.

When they published Gertrude Stein's *Autobiography of Alice Toklas,* Picasso and I were very disappointed because it was so full of lies.

I am opposed to writing about the private lives of living authors and psychoanalyzing them while they are alive. Criticism is getting all mixed up with a combination of the Junior FBI men, discards from Freud and Jung, and a sort of columnist peephole and missing laundry-list school. Every young English professor sees gold in them dirty sheets now. Imagine what they can do with the soiled sheets of four legal beds by the same writer, and you can see why their tongues are slavering.

In the old days I could read anything, but now I cannot read detective stories anymore unless they are written by Raymond Chandler.

WOMEN

When women have any feeling of guilt,

they tend to get rid of it by slapping it onto you.

Previous pages: Lunch with Ava Gardner, Matador Dominguín, Mary, and others, at tienta in Spain. Above, left to right: Mary; with Mary, Finca Vigía, Cuba, 1960. Opposite: With Mary, Finca Vigía.

What makes a woman good in bed makes it impossible for her to live alone. But not the tough ones. The tough ones like to live alone. Even when they're living with a man, they're living alone.

God knows I do not have a definitive reading on womenies, but I do know that little things count much more than big things. And it's all a question of balance. Too little sex, neglected; too much, you're oversexed; Christ, man should get changing readings on a woman's mood like he gets the *côtes jaunes* before each race. But don't try to find an untroublesome woman. She will dull out on you.

The only constructive thing I ever learned about women is no matter how they turned out, you should remember them only as they were on the best day they ever had.

Brett died in New Mexico [Lady Brett Ashley of *The Sun Also Rises*]. Call her Lady Duff Twysden, if you like, but I can only think of her as Brett. Tuberculosis. She was forty-three. Her pallbearers had all been her lovers. On leaving the church, where she had had a proper service, one of the grieving pallbearers slipped on the church steps and the casket dropped and split open.

Above: With his first wife, Hadley Richardson; her sister; and Ernest's mother. Opposite, left to right: with Pauline, San Sebastián, 1927; Hadley; Pauline Pfeiffer, Vogue writer, 1918.

Only one marriage I regret. I remember after I got that marriage license I went across from the license bureau to a bar for a drink. The bartender said, "What will you have, sir?" And I said, "A glass of hemlock."

Le Jockey was the best nightclub that ever was. Best orchestra, best drinks, a wonderful clientele, and the world's most beautiful women. Was in there one night when the place was set on fire by the most sensational woman anybody ever saw. Or ever will. Tall, coffee skin, ebony eyes, legs of paradise, a smile to end all smiles. Very hot night but she was wearing a coat of black fur, her breasts handling the fur like it was silk. She turned her eyes on me—she was dancing with the big British gunner subaltern who had brought her—but I responded to the eyes like a hypnotic and cut in on them. The subaltern tried to shoulder me out but the girl slid off him and onto me. Everything under that fur instantly communicated with me. I introduced myself and asked her name. "Josephine Baker," she said. We danced nonstop for the rest of the night. She never took off her fur coat. Wasn't until the joint closed she showed me she had nothing on underneath.

These Cuban girls, you look into their black eyes, they have hot sunlight in them.

LIFE

My luck, she is running very good.

As you get older, it is harder to have heroes, but more necessary.

My own ethics are only to attack on time and never leave your wounded except to pleasant auspices.

Love is infinitely more durable than hate.

Previous pages:
Churriana, Spain.
Right: En route
from Ketchum to
Key West, 1959.

When I was young I never wanted to get married, but after I did, I could never be without a wife again. Same about kids. I never wanted any, but after I had one, I never wanted to be without them. To be a successful father, though, there's one absolute rule: when you have a kid, don't look at it for the first two years.

Above, left to right: Working on For Whom the Bell Tolls, *Cuba; with Bumby, Paris, 1928. Following page (inset): Sixtieth-birthday lunch, Málaga, Spain, July 21, 1959.*

You can have true affection for only a few things in life, and by getting rid of material things, I make sure I won't waste mine on something that can't feel my affection.

Did you ever see me leave a place with anything but reluctance?

Courage is a matter of one's conscience, not beholden to the evaluation of others.

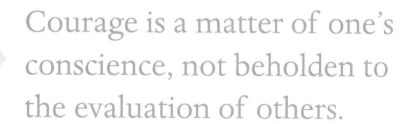

I gave up expensive wines for Lent of 1947, and never took it up again. Also gave up smoking long before that, because cigarette smoke is the nose's worst enemy, and how can you enjoy a good wine that you cannot truly smell?

The day after *The Sun Also Rises* was published, I got word that Harold Loeb, who was the Robert Cohn of the book, had announced that he would kill me on sight. I sent him a telegram to the effect that I would be in Le Trou dans le Mur for three consecutive evenings, so he'd have no trouble finding me. I chose this joint because it is all mirrors, all four walls, and if you sit in a booth at the back you can see whoever comes in the door and all their moves. I waited out the three days but Harold didn't show. About a week later, I was eating dinner at Lipp's in Saint-Germain, which is also heavily mirrored, when I spotted Harold coming in. I went over and put out my hand, and Harold started to shake hands before he remembered we were mortal enemies. He yanked his hand away and put it behind his back. I invited him to have a drink, but he refused. "Never," is actually what he said. "Okay," I said, resuming my seat, "then drink alone." He left the restaurant, and that was the end of that vendetta. What ruined poor Loeb was that he was an authentic Guggenheim, but he never got one of his recommendations approved. Not one. There's rejection for you, in spades.

Top: Le Trou dans le Mur. Above: Harold Loeb, 1922. Opposite: Sloppy Joe's.

I know a Basque who is a prolific letter writer, and each letter ends the same way—"Send money."

❋

I don't like to go to other people's houses, because I can't trust the food and drink. The last time I accepted a dinner invitation was about a year ago. They served sweet champagne, which I had to drink to be polite, and it look ten days for me to get it out of my system.

❋

I used to be co-owner of Sloppy Joe's. Silent partner, they call it. We had gambling in the back, and that's where the real money was. But getting good dice-changers was difficult because if he was so good, you couldn't detect it yourself, you knew he would steal from you. The only big expense in a gambling operation, ours included, is police protection. We paid $7,500 to elect a sheriff who, in his second year in office, went God-happy on us and closed us down, so we closed down the sheriff.

I may wear a beard, but when you look close, I ain't Santa Claus.

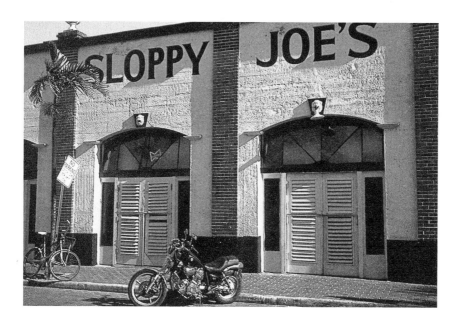

Drinking is fun, not a release from something. When it's a release from something, except the straight mechanical pressure that we are all subjected to always, then I think you get to be a rummy. But I am not a first-stone caster.

※

I've been drunk one thousand, five hundred and forty-seven times in my life, but never in the morning.

※

You can tell me how to write, shoot, or make love, but you cannot tell me how to enter a harbor.

※

I ride a good race when the going is not good, and when things are really bad you can count on me, complete with defects, to ride a better race than if it was easy.

※

We stood there, helplessly watching the de Havilland burn up, and I made several scientific notations that might interest students of the alcoholic occult. First noted there were four little pops, which I chalked up as belonging to our four bottles of Carlsberg beer. Then there was a more substantial pop, which I credited to the bottle of Grand Macnish. But the only really good bang came from the Gordon's gin. It was an unopened bottle with a metal top. The Grand Macnish was corked and besides was half gone. But the Gordon's had real éclat.

※

Opposite: Crash of the Cessna, Africa. Opposite (inset): Worldwide obits.

They've slowed me down but they haven't stopped me. They'd have to chop off both legs at the knees and nail me to the stake for that—but even then I could probably still get them with my reflex action.

When I picked myself up off the floor of the second plane [crash in Africa], I felt busted inside. The rear door was bent and jammed. My right arm and shoulder were dislocated, but I used my left shoulder and my head and had good pushing room to get it open. Roy Marsh, the pilot, was up front with Miss Mary. I yelled to him, "I have it open here. Miss Mary okay?" Was glad to see Miss Mary without a scratch on her and carrying her vanity case. Never been in a crisis yet that a woman forgot her jewels.

HEMINGWAY, WIFE KILLED IN AIR CRASH

'NO SIGN OF LIFE' AT WRECK ...

Miró and I were good friends; we were working hard, but neither of us was selling anything. My stories would all come back with rejection slips, and Miró's unsold canvases were piled up all over his studio. There was one I had fallen in love with—a painting of his farm down south—it haunted me and even though I was broke, I wanted to own it, but since we were such good friends, I insisted that we do it through a dealer. So we gave the picture to a dealer and, knowing he had a sure sale, he put a price of two hundred dollars on it, damn steep, but I arranged to pay it off in six installments. The dealer made me sign a chattel mortgage so that if I defaulted on any payment, I would lose the painting and all money paid in. Well, I skimped and managed okay until the last payment. I hadn't sold any stories or articles and I didn't have a franc to my name. I asked the dealer for an extension but, of course, he preferred to keep my dough *and* the painting.

That's where the Closerie des Lilas comes in. The day the dough was due, I came in there sad-ass for a drink. The barman asked me what was wrong, and I told him about the painting. He quietly passed the word around to the waiters and they raised the money for me out of their own pockets.

Above, left: Luxembourg pigeons. Above, right: Ernest's favorite café. Opposite, left: One of the cafés where Ernest liked to write. Opposite, right: Jardin du Luxembourg.

Am very fond of the Jardin du Luxembourg because it kept us from starvation. On days when the dinner pot was absolutely devoid of content, I would put Bumby, then about a year old, into the baby carriage and wheel him over to the Jardin. There was always a gendarme on duty, but I knew that about four o'clock he would go to a bar across from the park to have a glass of wine. That's when I would appear with Mr. Bumby—and a pocketful of corn for the pigeons. I would sit on a bench, in my guise of buggy-pushing pigeon-lover, casing the flock for clarity of eye and plumpness. The Luxembourg was well known for the classiness of its pigeons. Once my selection was made, it was a simple matter to entice my victim with the corn, snatch him, wring his neck, and flip his carcass under Mr. Bumby's blanket. We got a little tired of pigeon that winter, but they filled many a void.

I can't think of any better way to spend money than on champagne.

I don't distinguish between Jews and non-Jews, because I can't tell a Jew from anyone else.

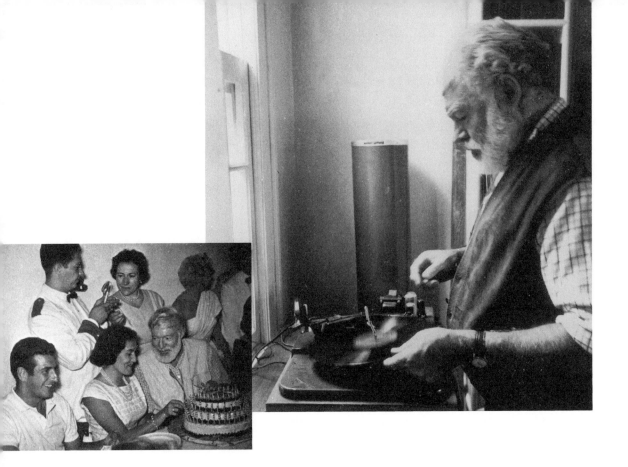

Above, left: Sixtieth birthday party, Churriana, Spain. Above, right: Finca Vigía turntable.

Back in the old days, Harry's New York Bar on rue Daunou was one of the few good, solid bars, and there was an ex-pug used to come in with a pet lion. He'd stand at the bar here and the lion would stand here beside him. He was a very nice lion with good manners—no growls or roars—but, as lions will, he occasionally shit on the floor. This, of course, had a rather adverse effect on the trade and, as politely as he could, Harry asked the ex-pug not to bring the lion around anymore. But the next day the pug was back with lion, lion dropped another load, drinkers dispersed, Harry again made request. The third day, same thing. Realizing it was do or die for poor Harry's business, this time when lion let go, I went over, picked up the pug, who had been a welterweight, carried him outside, and threw him in the street. Then I came back and grabbed the lion's mane and hustled him out of there. Out on the sidewalk the lion gave me a look, but he went quietly.

> Man is not made for defeat.
> Man can be destroyed
> but not defeated.

Scott Fitzgerald came to visit me. Scott was staying at the Ritz, as usual. He brought his little daughter, Scotty, with him. While we were talking, Scotty announced she wanted to make pee-pee, but when I told Scott the W.C. was on the floor below, he told Scotty that was too far to go and to do it in the hall. The concierge observed the trickle coming down the steps and went upstairs to inquire. "Monsieur," he said to Scott very politely, "would it not be more comfortable for Mademoiselle to use the W.C.?" Scott said, "Back to your miserable room, concierge, or I will put your head in the W.C." He was mad as hell. He came back into my room and began stripping off the wallpaper, which was old and starting to peel. I begged him not to because, as always, I was behind in my rent, but he was too mad to listen. The landlord made me pay for repapering the entire room. But Scott was my friend, and you put up with a lot in the name of a friendship.

I love all music, even opera. But I have no talent for it and cannot sing. I have a perfect goddamn ear for music, but I can't play any instrument by ear, not even the piano. My mother took me out of school one year to learn the cello, when I wanted to be out in the fresh air playing football. She wanted to have chamber music in the house.

Discipline is much more desirable than inspiration.

If you anticipate failure you'll have it. Of course, you are aware of what will happen if you fail, and you plan your escape routes—you would be unintelligent if you didn't—but you don't anticipate failure in the thing you do. Now, I don't want you to think I've never been spooked, but if you don't take command of your fears, no attack will ever go.

Style is not just an idle concept. It is simply a way to get done what is supposed to be done. The fact that the right way also looks beautiful when it's done is just incidental.

Below: Roman amphitheater, Nîmes, 1949. Opposite: Wyoming, 1933.

When I'm not going good, I go off where I can be alone and work the fat off my soul the way a fighter goes up into the mountains to work and train and burn the fat out of his body. Being alone and loneliness are two different things. I'll be alone but I won't be lonely.

Who said a dilemma had only two horns? He must have been fooling around with little dilemmas before they were of age. A real dilemma has between eight and ten pairs of horns and can kill you as far as you can see it and vice versa.

The Duke and Duchess of Windsor visited us in Cuba but they only seemed fascinated by the falling plaster.

I don't want to be an art critic. I just want to look at pictures and be happy with them and learn from them.

I think body and mind are closely coordinated. Fattening of the body can lead to fattening of the mind. I would be tempted to say that it can lead to fattening of the soul, but I don't know anything about the soul.

Never bet on any animal that can talk except yourself.

There's a fine old Spanish proverb that I learned from the great matador Belmonte: With patience and saliva, the elephant fucketh the ant.

Good times should be orchestrated and not left
to the uncertainties of chance.

Never confuse movement with action.

Things in the night are different than they are in the day, and there is no way to explain what differentiates them, because those night things disappear in the daylight, which is especially true of lonely people when they are in the grips of their loneliness.

Manet could show the bloom people have when they're still innocent and before they've been disillusioned.

Deviousness is permissible if it is innocuous.

Anger and compassion are not too far apart, and whenever possible, spent anger should give way to compassion.

Opposite: In Cuba, with a cat named Boise. Left: At the doorway of his Ketchum house.

Pride is a desirable trait that rescues one from a fall and not vice versa.

True friendship requires forgiveness, but no friendship can withstand the abuse of duplicity.

Old as I am, I continue to be amazed at the sudden emergence of daffodils and short stories.

Hesitation increases in relation to risk in equal proportion to age.

If you get too self-conscious, you get self-centered. Then follows selfishness, snobbery, artificiality, pretention, and postering, all worthless.

I never trust a doctor I have to pay.

When the famous become infamous it's pathetic.

There is an old Spanish saying: "The wind off the Escorial couldn't blow out a candle but it can kill a man."

Sometimes I write in my dreams, actual lines, and when that happens I wake myself up and write it down or I will have dreamed it all out.

A man should know how to get out of the doghouse or turn in his suit.

When people talk, listen completely. Most people never listen.

A motorcycle is okay until you hit gravel.

Opposite, left: Frolicking on the Riviera. Opposite, right: Living room, Finca Vigía. Left: In Mexico.

I get so bloody tired of sounding like me that I sometimes invent ways of not sounding like me. Sometimes I leave out the nouns. Sometimes the verbs. Sometimes the whole goddamn sentence. As a writer I put them all in, but when I've just finished a book and come to New York for a few days to see friends and have fun and be irresponsible, I can do what I want and say what I want.

Every Christmas I give all of my presents away, because I'm convinced that you don't own anything until you give it away.

I have seen all the sunrises there have been in my life.

If I live to be an old man, what I want to be is a wise old man who won't bore. I'd like to see all the new fighters, horses, ballets, dames, bullfighters, painters, airplanes, café characters, big international whores, restaurants, years of wine, and never have to write a line about any of it. And I would like to be able to make love good until I was eighty-five.

Previous pages:
Beside the Irati River,
Pamplona, 1957.
Above: One bear
Ernest didn't shoot.

If you are lucky enough to have lived in Paris as a young man, then wherever you go for the rest of your life, it stays with you, for Paris is a movable feast.

All things truly wicked start from an innocence.

Always do sober what you said you'd do drunk. That will teach you to keep your mouth shut.

An intelligent man is sometimes forced to be drunk to spend time with fools.

I have drunk since I was fifteen and few things have given me more pleasure. When you work hard all day with your head and know you must work again the next day, what else can change your ideas and make them run on a different plane like whiskey? When you are cold and wet, what else can warm you? Before an attack, who can say anything that gives you the momentary well-being that rum does? The only time it isn't good for you is when you write or when you fight. You have to do that cold. But it always helps my shooting. Modern life, too, is often a mechanical oppression, and liquor is the only mechanical relief.

The world breaks everyone, and afterward, some are strong at the broken places.

The best ammunition against lies is the truth, but there is no ammunition against gossip.

Happiness in intelligent people is the rarest thing I know.

I never played roulette that I didn't quit when I was well ahead.

There are those who urge me to take life seriously; if I ever do, a lot of characters will hang by their necks until dead.

The world is a fine place and worth the fighting for,

and I hate very much to leave it.

DEATH

I've been asked if there's anything I will regret before I die. Regret is a luxury for those who think they're going to live again. Forget all the fancy crap: courage—dignity—regret; cojones, that's all you need to die right. Cojones.

Previous pages: Burial, Ketchum, 1961. Opposite: Finca Vigía, 1960. The last picture Hotchner took of Hemingway.

Have I had an analyst? Sure I have. Portable Corona number three. That's been my analyst. I'll tell you, even though I am not a believer in the analysis, I spend a hell of a lot of time killing animals and fish so I won't kill myself. When a man is in rebellion against death, as I am in rebellion against death, he gets pleasure out of taking to himself one of the godlike attributes, that of giving it.

All stories end in death, and he is no true storyteller who would keep that from you.

It takes a pretty good man to make any sense when he's dying.

I think I will adopt a *nom de mort*. Why die under my own name? I wrote under my own name but I don't have to die under it. I shall die under the name of Steve Ketchel. How's that for a *nom de mort*?

Fear of death increases in exact proportion to increase in wealth: Hemingstein's Law on the dynamics of dying.

If I were reborn, and I had a choice, I'd be a Mormon.

Death is just another whore.

It has been emphasized that I have sought death all my life. If you have spent your life avoiding death as cagily as possible, but on the other hand taking no backchat from her and studying her as you would a beautiful harlot who could put you soundly to sleep forever with no problems and no necessity to work, you could be said to have studied her, but you have not sought her. Because you know among one or two other things that if you sought her, you would possess her, and from her reputation you know that she would present you with an incurable disease. So much for the constant pursuit of death.

What if you can no longer measure up, no longer be involved, if you have used up all your fantasies? A champion cannot retire like anyone else. How the hell can a writer retire? The public won't let him. When a man loses the center of his being, then he loses his being. Retire? It's the filthiest word in the English language. It's backing up into the grave. If I can't exist on my own terms, then existence is impossible. That is how I *have* lived and *must* live—or not live.

When I dream of afterlife in heaven, the action always takes place in the Paris Ritz. It's a fine summer night. I knock back a couple of martinis in the bar, Cambon side. Then there's a wonderful dinner under a flowering chestnut tree in what's called Le Petit Jardin. That's the little garden that faces the Grill. After a few brandies, I wander up to my room and slip into one of those huge Ritz beds. They are all made of brass. There's a bolster for my head the size of the Graf Zeppelin and four square pillows filled with real goose feathers—two for me, and two for my quite heavenly companion.

Above: Juárez, Mexico, 1955. Opposite: El Escorial, Spain, 1958.

Every man's life ends the same way, and it is only the details of how he lived and how he died that distinguish one man from another.

ACKNOWLEDGMENTS

Thanks to those at the John F. Kennedy Hemingway Collection, especially the photographic collection personnel, for their pleasant and thorough assistance. The same can be said of people at the Library of Congress, who have hundreds of Hemingway photos in their archives. Thanks also to Abigail Holstein, who with patience and impressive skill edited this book. I am grateful to Jack Hemingway, who, before his untimely death, suggested that I produce this book memorializing the wisdom of his father.

PERMISSIONS

Photograph of Gertrude Stein and Alice Toklas, page 82, courtesy of the Granger Collection, New York.

Photographs of William Faulkner and F. Scott Fitzgerald, pages 84–85, courtesy of the Library of Congress

Photograph of James Joyce, page 86, courtesy of Hulton Archive/Getty Images.

All other photographs are courtesy of the author, with additional grateful acknowledgment to:

The Hemingway Collection at the John F. Kennedy Library, Boston

The Hemingway Collection at the Library of Congress

Oak Park Historical Society

The photographers Cano and Roberto Sotolongo.

ABOUT THE EDITOR

A. E. Hotchner was born and raised in St. Louis, where he received his LLB and his doctor of law at Washington University. After practicing law for two years, Hotchner entered the Air Force, served with the Anti-Submarine Command, and emerged four years later a major.

Mr. Hotchner did not return to his practice in St. Louis but instead settled in New York City, where, as a freelance writer, he wrote more than 300 articles and short stories for such publications as *Esquire*, *Saturday Evening Post*, the *New York Times*, and *Reader's Digest*. During the golden days of television, when *Playhouse 90* flourished, he wrote a series of distinguished plays, including prizewinning adaptations of Ernest Hemingway's "The Snows of Kilimanjaro," "The Killers," and "The Fifth Column." He wrote the screenplay for *Adventures of a Young Man*, which starred Paul Newman.

Hotchner also wrote about his long friendship with Hemingway in *Papa Hemingway*, a highly acclaimed best-seller that was published in thirty-four countries in twenty-eight different languages. Mr. Hotchner has also written best-selling biographies of Doris Day and Sophia Loren. Two of Hotchner's books—*The Man Who Lived at the Ritz* and *Looking for Miracles*—were dramatized on television, and his memoir of his St. Louis boyhood, *King of the Hill*, was produced as a feature film. Hotchner also wrote *Blown Away*, a book about the 1960s and the Rolling Stones; a historical novel, *Louisiana Purchase*; a World

War II memoir, *The Day I Fired Alan Ladd*; *Everyone Comes to Elaine's*; *Dear Papa, Dear Hotch*; and *The Boyhood Memoirs of A.E. Hotchner*.

Hotchner has also written for theater. His play *The White House*, starring Helen Hayes, was performed on Broadway, and in 1996 it was performed in the East Room of the White House for President and Mrs. Clinton and an audience of distinguished guests. In 1993, a musical that Hotchner wrote with Cy Coleman, *Welcome to the Club*, was also performed on Broadway. In addition, Hotchner wrote *A Short Happy Life*, starring Rod Steiger; *The Hemingway Hero*, which starred Gary Merrill; and *Sweet Prince*, with Keir Dullea. A musical he wrote with the composer Cy Coleman, *Exactly Like You*, was performed at New York's York Theatre in 1999.

Along with his writing career, Hotch's accidental business venture with his longtime friend Paul Newman (whose first starring role was in *The Battler*, Hotchner's first television play) has turned into one of the country's surprising success stories. Their Newman's Own products generate millions of dollars of annual profit, which is entirely contributed to a long list of deserving charities. One of the beneficiaries is the Hole in the Wall Gang Camp, which they built in Connecticut for children with cancer and other life-threatening diseases. They have sponsored sister camps in Florida, New York State, California, and North Carolina, and internationally in France, Ireland, Israel, Italy, Hungary, and Africa.

BOSTON PUBLIC LIBRARY

3 9999 06515 695 0